Safe To

The current and future use of secure accommodation for children and young people

The National Children's Bureau was established as a registered charity in 1963. Our purpose is to identify and to promote the interests of all children and young people and to improve their status in a diverse society.

We work closely with professionals and policy makers to improve the lives of all children but especially children under five, those affected by family instability and children with special needs or disabilities.

We collect and disseminate information about children and promote good practice in children's services through research, policy and practice development, publications, seminars, training and an extensive library and information service.

The Bureau works in partnership with Children in Scotland and Children in Wales.

ISBN 1 874579 63 6

Published by National Children's Bureau Enterprises Ltd, 8 Wakley Street, London EC1V 7QE. Telephone 0171 843 6000.

National Children's Bureau Enterprises is the trading company for the National Children's Bureau (registered charity number 258825).

Typeset by Books Unlimited (Nottm), NG19 7QZ.

Printed and bound in the United Kingdom by Redwood Books, Wiltshire BA 14 8RN

Contents

Foreword

The original discussion paper which led to this book was written by Rachel Hodgkin (Principal Policy Officer at the National Children's Bureau); the analysis of data from the survey was conducted by Ann Mason.

Funding for the survey, discussion groups and this report was donated by William A Cadbury Charitable Trust and the Percy Bilton Charity, to whom the Bureau gives grateful thanks.

The conclusions of this report are those of the National Children's Bureau; the views expressed by the discussion group are not necessarily shared by the Bureau.

1. Introduction

Little official information is given about the children who are held in secure units – locally managed locked units for children in care or on remand who are deemed unsafe to keep in open accommodation, and for children who have committed the most serious offences. For example, neither the Social Services Inspectorate nor the annually published Government statistics on children in secure units provide full information on what behaviour has caused the children to be locked up. With generous support from two independent and charitable foundations, the National Children's Bureau sought fuller information on this crucial point and on other aspects of secure accommodation for young people.

This report draws on a snapshot survey of children locked in secure units on 31 March 1994 and from the discussions of a group of professionals working in – mostly managing – secure accommodation. The survey findings included here are those relevant to the general discussion; a copy of the full questionnaire is appended: details of the findings from it are available on request from the National Children's Bureau. The report also uses statistical and policy-related information provided by the Department of Health, as well as drawing on the existing body of research in this area.

The report focuses on the justifications for locking up children and on the current operation of secure accommodation (that is, social services-based locked units for children); the last section draws some tentative conclusions. While professionals working in secure accommodation are an undeniably partial and subjective source of information on the general issue under discussion – the locking up of children – they offer an important, and little heard, perspective. Their views reported here, though not necessarily shared by the Bureau, certainly suggest – as we recommend – that current provisions for locking up children urgently need a serious and thorough-going review.

We make one firm recommendation on page 56:

That the Government should, as a matter of urgency, convene a major review of all law and policy (penal, health and social services) relating to the locking up of children with a view to securing the aim of Article 37 of the UN Convention on the Rights of the Child – that the child should be locked up only as a last resort and for the shortest appropriate time.

We follow this with preliminary conclusions which could well be reinforced or modified when published alongside conclusions that emerge from perspectives other than those of the Unit Managers. The important thing is that this work starts now.

Internationally agreed principles

The policy objective of this report (and of the National Children's Bureau) is to contribute to the debate on what should be done with children who appear to need to be locked up, in order that the following undertaking in the UN Convention on the Rights of the Child, is met:

... The arrest, detention or imprisonment of the child ... shall be used only as a measure of last resort and for the shortest appropriate period of time. (Article 37 of the UN Convention on the Rights of the Child, ratified by the UK in 1991).

The treatment of juvenile delinquents (that is, unacceptably troublesome children under the age of 18) is also addressed in three other international instruments, all accepted by the UK: *The UN Standard Minimum Rules for the Administration of Juvenile Justice 1985* (The Beijing Rules), *The United Nations Guidelines for the Prevention of Juvenile Delinquency 1990* (The Riyadh Guidelines) and the *United Nations Rules for the Protection of Juveniles Deprived of their Liberty 1990*. Some of the statements of principle from these instruments, relevant to this report, are set out below:

Restrictions on deprivation of liberty

- deprivation of a juvenile's liberty shall be a disposition of last resort, for the minimum necessary period and should be limited to exceptional cases;
- deprivation of liberty should not be imposed unless the juvenile is adjudicated of a serious act involving violence against another person or of persistence in committing other serious offences and unless there is no other appropriate remedy;

- a judicial authority shall determine the length of the sanction without precluding the possibility of early release;

Remands to custody

- detention before trial shall be avoided as far as possible and limited to exceptional circumstances;
- priority shall be given to expediting the case to ensuring the shortest possible period of detention;
- untried detainees should be separated from convicted juveniles;

Treatment in locked units

- where time permits individual treatment plans shall be drawn up for all detained juveniles;
- all locked units must ensure that the children are protected from harmful influences or risk situations;
- the principal criterion for the separation of different categories of locked-up juveniles should be the provision of the type of care best suited to their particular needs and the protection of their physical, mental and moral integrity and well-being;
- 'open' detention facilities (that is, those with minimum or no security measures) should be provided as well as 'closed';
- all detention facilities should be small-scale, integrated into the social, economic and cultural environment and easily accessible by the juveniles' family;
- detention facility staff should be qualified and include specialists such as educators, vocational instructors, counsellors, social workers, psychiatrists and psychologists;

Prevention

- the successful prevention of juvenile delinquency requires efforts on the part of the whole of society; in particular laws, processes, institutions, facilities and a service delivery network should be aimed at reducing the motivation, need and opportunity for or conditions giving rise to delinquency;
- consideration should be given to the fact that a lot of youthful misbehaviour disappears spontaneously on transition to adulthood and the fact that labelling young people can contribute to the development of consistent patterns of delinquency;
- preventive services should include community involvement, inter-departmental cooperation, family support (including

parent education about children's needs) and an education system that encourages tolerance and personal responsibility;
- generally participation in prevention plans should be voluntary and young people should be involved in their formulation, development and implementation.

There seems to be a growing consensus, within the voluntary sector at least, that if children have to be locked up then this should be done in local authority secure accommodation, often identified as centres of excellence. A common perception is that these small, often mixed-sex, local, well-staffed social services-run locked units which aim to treat not punish and to lock up only for the necessary minimum period make a striking contrast with the locked institutions existing within the penal system. NACRO, The Children's Society, NCH Action for Children, the Howard League for Penal Reform and others agree that penal custody for children and young people should be phased out. Relevant professional bodies and opposition parties have also expressed tentative support for this view, as has the Home Affairs Select Committee (which called for a Home Office feasibility study into this in its sixth report[1]). International law and guidance also endorse the use of welfare-based locked placements for children (see pages 2 and 3).

But if the secure accommodation system is to have sole responsibility for locking up children then a great deal more thought, energy and resources need to be spent on its administration and legislation, as well as on the wider systems of support and prevention.

The report shows that secure units currently lock up a comprehensively wide range of children, including suicidal children, drug abusers, child prostitutes, runaways, petty offenders, dangerous and violent children, children on remand and those who have committed extremely serious offences.

The findings suggest that many of the children now locked up in secure accommodation need not be there, and that the unnecessary locking up of children and massive geographical inconsistencies which exist at present are likely to grow worse with the forthcoming increase in secure places, the 'demonopolising' (privatising) of secure units, the new powers of courts and financial incentives to place children in secure accommodation, not to mention media and political pressures.

For example the survey shows:

- the secure unit managers completing the form considered that

60 children out of the 193 children surveyed could have been safely accommodated in open accommodation;

- these 60 children exhibited a very wide range of behaviours meriting placement in a secure unit, including extremely serious offending and extremely serious forms of self-harm;
- the managers were also asked where these children might have been placed safely. Their responses suggest that there are serious deficiencies in residential care and other alternatives;
- the survey shows an uneven, potentially discriminatory, distribution of children within the units. In terms of geography, two authorities locked up twice as many children on the survey day (11 and ten children) than any other authority; eight out of the top ten authorities in this list also manage their own units. In terms of gender, although there are fewer girls than boys overall, girls outnumber boys in the numbers being locked up for their own, rather than others', safety. In terms of ethnicity, black Caribbean and African children were disproportionately represented within the units on the survey day; Asian children were under-represented;
- 82% of the children in the units were locked up under the Children Act ground relating to absconding, but the survey suggests that there is no agreed working definition of 'absconding';

This report also includes the following points made by the professional discussion group:

- there were significant numbers of children for whom secure accommodation could be little help (or could even be counterproductive);
- secure unit staff play an important but generally unrecognised role in filtering out unsuitable candidates for a secure placement;
- the mental health services are abdicating responsibility for children in secure units, particularly violent children;
- the privatisation of secure units is likely to lead to more children being locked up unnecessarily.

Retribution, deterrence, containment and danger to self or others

It is agreed by all that some children have to be locked up. The reasons for locking up children in the penal and welfare services at present fall under five rough headings: for retribution, for deterrence, for containment in order to prevent them reoffending, because they are a danger to others and because they are a danger to themselves. Children are of course often locked up under more than one, or all, of these headings.

A striking example of retribution can be found in the treatment of the killers of James Bulger. Their trial, identification and 15-year minimum sentence reflected a public desire for vengeance on a scale unprecedented for many decades. The boys' chances of developing into normal, sociable, productive citizens have of course been drastically diminished by such treatment. Although there seems little likelihood that they will kill again (no case appears to exist of an under 16-year-old murderer killing again) all the evidence suggests that long incarceration of children and young people, however benign, leads to mental health problems, petty criminality and debilitating institutionalisation.[2] The notoriety of this particular case and the identification of the boys and their families will of course make any 'normalisation' almost impossible.

The desire of our society for retribution – to make offenders suffer for their sins – goes counter to our more rational, more self-preserving, desire to rehabilitate. In the current climate, arguing against a punishment-based response to offending may appear naive – but the fact remains that retribution plays no part in the international charters quoted on pages 2 and 3 and should play no part in our domestic policy on juvenile crime.

The need for custody as a deterrent also has widespread support in this country. One of the primary defining characteristics of juvenile offenders is a failure to perceive the consequences of their actions and a tendency to act impulsively, without forethought.[3] The deterrent intention of a custodial sentence would therefore seem to be particularly ineffective for this group. The **experience** of custody certainly has a poor record in deterring reoffending, as every analysis of subsequent offending patterns of children leaving custody has consistently shown.

Custody simply as a measure of containment, just to keep the children off the streets where they have been doing damage to themselves and others, is superficially attractive in a minimalist and depressing way. However too much evidence exists to show that locking up children does not just contain them in a state of suspended animation, it often makes their offending or self-destructive behaviour more serious. A policy of containment is one pursued at our peril.

So when might the locking up of children be justified? At first sight the criteria for placement in secure accommodation set out in Section 25 of the Children Act 1989 seem unarguable:

> A child... may not be placed, and, if placed, may not be kept, in accommodation provided for the purpose of restricting liberty ('secure accommodation') unless it appears–
>
> (a) that–
>> (i) he has a history of absconding and is likely to abscond from any other description of accommodation; and
>> (ii) if he absconds, he is likely to suffer significant harm;
>
> or
>
> (b) that if he is kept in any other description of accommodation he is likely to injure himself or other persons.'

However these conditions beg a number of question. For example, why exactly is it necessary to lock up young people who are only a risk to themselves? What if their behaviour is untreatable within the locked placement? What about those who are refused bail and would, if they were adults, be remanded in custody? What about young people who are not likely to injure others but persistently steal or damage property? Is it legitimate to lock up a child if 'other description of accommodation' (such as, open accommodation) **could** be used but is not, for whatever reason, available? Would it be justified to hold an extremely dangerous young person on an indefinite basis? How can one determine which to lock up of the many thousands of young people whose behaviours make them eligible for security – car thieves for instance, or runaways? What filters, judicial or otherwise, ensure that **only** the necessary minimum are locked up?

These questions are raised by the findings of this report. Current policy and practice do not offer satisfactory answers.

2. Information on which the report is based

The survey of children

The questionnaire was sent to 27 units (or 29 if Aycliffe Centre's and Redbank's two secure units are counted separately). Replies were received from 24 units, though one only to say that it had closed. Three units did not respond. Information on 200 children within the units on 31 March 1994 was sent, but the information on seven children was flawed and had to be discounted.

By the time of writing the Department of Health had fortunately published its own annual statistics on children in secure units[4], which includes a similar snapshot survey of the units' population at that date as well as information about the previous year. Missing information can therefore be deduced from the Department's figures, though there are some variations between our figures and the Government figures.

The Department's figures derive from a single-form return from each unit; the units completed a fairly lengthy questionnaire on each child for the Bureau. The Department's statistics give details of 51 children in the units on 31 March 1994 not included in our survey. 36 were from the three units which did not respond (East Moor Children's Centre in Leeds, Orchard Lodge in Southwark and 125C Market Street Children's Centre in Derbyshire). Seven were the flawed returns. The Department also had information on an additional four children from Aycliffe Centre, two from Dyson Hall Children's Home, one from Briars Hey Children's Centre and one from Frant Court. There are also some discrepancies between the two surveys as regards legal status which probably resulted from the complexities surrounding legal status, particularly whether a child has been remanded or is being looked after (the Bureau returns show more children who are on remand).

The two youth treatment centres Glenthorne and St Charles, which lock up similar categories of children, were not included in the survey. They too produced figures on the 60 children accommodated on 31 March 1994, which provided useful background material.

Finally there are the unknown numbers of children who are locked up, subject to Section 25 of the Children Act, in NHS and private medical establishments or are accommodated by local education authorities. No information is sought or provided by the Government on these children though the Children Act (Secure Accommodation) Regulations legalised this use of secure accommodation in 1991. Within the health sector it is known that the Gardener adolescent psychiatric unit and Ashworth secure special hospital (NHS) and St. Andrews (private) lock up children but there could well be more. No information is available on the use of secure accommodation in schools. More information is urgently needed on the use of secure accommodation: providing a complete picture of all children who are locked up, in whatever type of institution, must surely come near the top of the list.

This report does not consider, except tangentially, children locked up in penal establishments governed by the Home Office such as young offender institutions and remand wings of adult prisons.

The professional viewpoint

There are many professionals involved in the locking up of children. Local authority social services have responsibility for determining when children looked after and remanded to care meet the legal criteria for secure accommodation under the Children Act; magistrates have the responsibility for approving placements beyond 72 hours, and will in future be able to require a secure placement for remanded children. Judges and the Home Secretary have responsibility for the sentencing and placement of grave offenders. But of all the professionals who deal with these extremely troubled children, the ones who perhaps have the closest and longest relationship with them and certainly the ones who encounter the largest number of such children are those who are working in the locked units. Yet more attention is paid to the views of magistrates, court clerks, social workers, police and probation than to the views of this group. It therefore seemed useful to find out some of what they think.

In addition to factual information the questionnaire sought the subjective view of the manager completing it as to whether each individual child could, either at the time of admission or on the date of the survey, have been safely accommodated in open provision and if so, where?

Alongside the survey, the National Children's Bureau held four meetings between May and November 1994 with a group of managers of secure units and professionals working in the Youth Treatment Service (the two Youth Treatment Centres were set up by the Department of Health rather than by local authorities, but take similar categories of children to regional secure units). In total there were ten members of the group, including a manager of a large regional secure unit for boys, managers of three medium sized mixed units, one small girls-only unit and one small mixed unit, and two psychologists, one senior social worker and one teacher from the youth treatment service. On average, four to five members attended the meetings. The discussions were illuminating, thought-provoking and sometimes alarming. It should however be made quite clear that the views and conclusions of this report are those of the National Children's Bureau and not of this group.

Finally, officials from the Department of Health kindly answered questions about central government plans and policy relating to secure accommodation.

The law: legal grounds for locking up children in secure units

The National Children's Bureau conducted this research because the Department of Health statistics, useful though they are, do not reveal *why* the children are locked up. Figures are collected about individual children's legal status. This is helpful but knowing that children are under a care order does not tell you whether, for example, they are being locked up because they are violent or self-mutilating or runaways or fire-setters and so forth. We therefore asked detailed questions about how the children met the legal grounds for locking them up.

Children who are being looked after by the local authority (or who are remanded or detained in local authority accommodation) may be locked in secure accommodation under **Section 25 of the Children Act 1989** for the following reasons:

Section 25 of the Children Act 1989

Children who are looked after (or who are remanded or detained to local authority accommodation but who do not meet Regulation 6 criteria, see below) may only be locked or kept in secure accommodation:

- *because they have a 'history of absconding' (undefined), are likely to abscond from 'any other description of accommodation' and if they abscond are likely to suffer 'significant harm' (defined under Section 31 of the Act as including harm to physical, intellectual, emotional, social or behavioural development, 'significant' turning on a comparison with what could be expected of a similar child);*
- *because they might injure themselves if kept in any other description of accommodation;*
- *because they might injure other persons if kept in any other description of accommodation.*

The care authority has primary responsibility for deciding if these criteria are met and if so, whether the child needs to be placed in secure accommodation. Magistrates will then have to approve any placement of over 72 hours (or 72 aggregated over 28 days).

Section 25 grounds are modified under **Regulation 6 of the Children (Secure Accommodation) Regulations 1991:**

Regulation 6

If under 17-year-olds have been remanded to or detained in local authority accommodation and have:

either *been charged with or convicted of a sexual or violent offence or an offence punishable in an adult with a prison term of 14 years or more*

or *have a recent history of absconding while remanded to local authority accommodation and are charged with or has been convicted of an imprisonable offence when on remand*

then they can be locked up in secure accommodation under modified grounds of Section 25, as follows:

- *that any accommodation other than that which restricts their liberty (open accommodation) is inappropriate because they are likely to abscond from it;*
- *that open accommodation is inappropriate because they are likely to injure themselves;*
- *that open accommodation is inappropriate because they are likely to injure others.*

In other words they do not have to show a history of absconding, or that they will be at risk of significant harm when on the run. The numbers of remanded children in secure accommodation will significantly increase on full implementation of the 1991 Criminal Justice Act, which eliminates the placement of remanded 15 and

16-year-old boys in penal custody, and when the provisions in the 1994 Criminal Justice and Public Order Act enabling courts to remand 12 to 14-year-olds to secure accommodation also come into force.

Finally children are placed in secure units under **Section 53 of the Children and Young Persons Act 1933**. This is the sentence reserved for those children who are convicted of 'grave offences'. The Secretary of State (the Home Secretary) can determine where the young person is detained. In theory this could be anywhere, in practice it almost always means either secure accommodation or a young offender institution.

Section 53(1) is for murder. It provides an indefinite sentence, dependent on the Her Majesty's pleasure;

Section 53(2) allows fixed term or 'life' sentences for the remaining range of grave offences, defined as those offences which in the case of an adult carry a sentence of 14 years or more. This includes rape, robbery, aggravated burglary and arson. Only 14 to 17-year-olds were eligible for Section 53(2) sentences on March 31 1994: ten to 13-year-olds will become eligible when the Criminal Justice and Public Order Act 1994 is implemented. Such sentences are as a rule longer than the maximum term allowed for young offender institutions.

3. Findings from the survey

Legal status and age of the children

Out of the 193 children in our survey:

- 96 were locked up under Section 25 provisions (12 of which were on remand but did not appear to meet Regulation 6 criteria);
- 35 were (or appeared to be) locked up under Regulation 6;
- 62 were sentenced under section 53.

The youngest was a ten-year-old (held under Section 25) and there were seven 18-year-olds (all Section 53s); the peak age was 15.

What behaviour led to the placement?

Section 25 children

In the case of children placed under Section 25 more than one of its grounds could apply (see page 10). Of the 96 children:

Number of children	%	Legal ground for locked placement
40	41.7	A history of absconding, were likely to abscond from open accommodation and risked significant harm when on the run ('absconding')
22	22.9	Absconders *and* were likely to injure themselves in open accommodation ('self-injury') *and* were likely to injure others ('dangerous')
14	14.6	Absconding *and* self-injury
10	10.4	Self-injury *and* dangerous
6	6.2	Dangerous
3	3.1	Dangerous *and* absconding
1	1.1	Self-injury

The questionnaire also sought to know what behaviours had been identified as justifying the criteria. Of the 79 children who were absconders the question was asked: 'What significant harm was he or she likely to suffer?' 36 of these children were also self-injurers, but in addition there were the ten self-injuring and dangerous children and the one solely self-injuring child. Of these children the question was asked: 'In what way was he or she likely to injure him/herself?'

Putting together the answers to these two questions the following behaviours of the 90 self-injuring children were cited:

Number of children	%	Self-harming behaviour cited
11	12.5	Substance abuse (drugs, alcohol or solvents) *and* dangerous driving
9	10	Substance abuse
7	7.8	Substance abuse *and* criminal activities
7	7.8	Dangerous driving
6	6.6	Moral danger/prostitution *and* substance abuse
6	6.6	Female prostitution
6	6.6	Substance abuse *and* self-harm/suicidal activities
5	5.5	Suicide attempts
5	5.5	Self-harm
4	4.4	Moral danger
3	3.3	Dangerous driving *and* criminal activities
1	1.1	Male prostitution
2	2.2	Criminal activities
1	1.1	Retribution
1	1.1	Other ('Harm relating to serious sex offence charge')
6	6.6	Not specified
10	11.3	More than one of the above

It should perhaps be noted here that of the 96 children in all, at least 38 (38.5%) were not overtly dangerous to others.

As regards the 41 children who were deemed a danger to others the survey asked: 'In what way was he or she likely to injure other persons?' The answers were:

Number of children	%	Dangerous behaviour cited
16	39	Physical assault
13	31.7	Dangerous driving
4	9.7	Arson
3	7.3	Sexual assault
1	2.5	Recruiting prostitutes
3	7.3	More than one of the above
1	2.5	Not specified

In the case of all 96 children the authorities have to be satisfied that it appeared that the child could not be accommodated in 'any other description of accommodation'. In respect of each child the survey asked why it appeared no 'other description of accommodation' was able to prevent that behaviour.

When the absconding ground was cited the responses were examined to see if more than one type of placement had been tried. 27 (34.1%) indicated that they had. (For example: 'Mixture of children's homes and foster care tried', 'Numerous instances over several months from foster care, residential care, therapeutic community, placement with 1:1 supervision and return home'). Of the self-injurers, most responses on why open accommodation could not contain them (38.8%) referred to an absconding history or one where a number of alternatives had been tried (12.2%). 12.2% said that the level of staffing and resources in open accommodation was inadequate to prevent the self-injury and 8.2% mentioned the availability of the means to cause self-injury (windows, knives, pills and so on). As regards the dangerous children, the responses to the question why open accommodation was thought not to be possible showed roughly similar proportions of children with absconding histories or who had exhausted alternatives or whose behaviour could not be controlled by the resources in open provision, but 16.7% also suggested that the child was too inherently dangerous, for example 'injury impulsive and unpredictable', 'diagnosed as a pathological arsonist'.

Remanded children

12 of the children placed in secure units under **Section 25** had been remanded to local authority accommodation under Section 23 of the Children and Young Persons Act 1963. The identified reasons were:

Number of children	Legal ground for locked placement
7	Absconding *and* self-injury *and* dangerous
3	Absconding
1	Absconding *and* self-injury
1	Self-injurer *and* dangerous

Putting both dangerous and self-injuring behaviours together, the cited behaviours were:

Number of children	Dangerous and self-harming behaviours cited
7	Dangerous driving *and* substance abuse
2	Criminal activities (under 'risk of significant harm')
1	Substance abuse *and* history of assault
1	Substance abuse
1	Not known

35 children were identified by us as having been locked up under the modified grounds of **Regulation 6**. 15 of these were remanded children who had been entered in the Section 25 children's form, but as the answers made clear that it was the violent or sexual nature of the offence with which they had been charged that was the primary reason for the risk of injury to others they were re-categorised as Regulation 6 children.

Of these 35:

Number of children	%	Legal ground justifying locked placement
9	25.8	Dangerous
8	22.9	Absconding *and* self-injury *and* dangerous
7	21.0	Absconding
6	17.1	Absconding *and* dangerous
1	2.5	Absconding *and* self-injury
1	2.5	Self-injury *and* dangerous
1	2.5	Self injury
2	5.7	Not known

Of the 11 self-injurers the cited behaviours were:

Number of children	Self-injuring behaviour cited
4	Substance abuse
2	Arson
2	Retribution
1	Suicide
1	Arson and substance abuse
1	Not specified

Of the 24 dangerous children the cited behaviour was:

Number of children	Dangerous behaviour cited
16	Charged with a dangerous offence
3	History of violence
3	Might inflict reprisals on others
2	Arson

Children sentenced for grave offences under Section 53

62 children in the units were sentenced under Section 53 of the Children and Young Persons Act 1933 for 'grave crimes'. The offences they had committed were:

Number of children	%	Offence committed
15	24.1	Robbery
6	9.6	Arson
5	8.0	Aggravated burglary
4	6.5	Murder
4	6.5	Manslaughter
3	4.8	Rape
3	4.8	Attempted rape
2	3.2	Grievous bodily harm
2	3.2	Attempted robbery
1	1.6	Assault
1	1.6	Attempted murder
1	1.6	Kidnapping
1	1.6	Wounding
1	1.6	Incest
1	1.6	False imprisonment
10	16.5	More than one of the above
2	3.2	Not known

Could the children have been safely accommodated in open provision?

The unit manager, in respect of each Section 25 and Regulation 6 child, was asked:

> *In your opinion*, could the young person have been placed safely in some form of 'other description of accommodation' when he or she was admitted to the unit. If yes, what sort of accommodation?

and

> *In your opinion*, could the young person now be placed safely in some form of 'other description of accommodation?'

These questions relate to the legal criteria for placement under Section 25 and Regulation 6 (see pages 10 and 11).

As regards the Section 53 children, their term in custody was dependent on the Secretary of State since even under a fixed term sentence he has discretion to accommodate the child in an open setting. Although public safety is not the only factor in making his decision – he considers also the requirements of retribution and deterrence and the need to maintain public confidence in the system of justice – the unit managers were also asked:

> *In your opinion*, at the time of admission do you think the young person could have been safely accommodated in some sort of open provision?' (and the same question was repeated for 'now').

We asked that the principal officer of the unit should complete the form (or head of a section in the case of larger units). In virtually all cases it appears that the head of the unit filled it in, but in one case an off-site line manager who was technically 'Principal Officer' did the return. She wrote that it was quite inappropriate for her to answer many of the questions, particularly the ones which relied upon opinion.

A secure unit head at of one of the units which were not included in the survey had another, more interesting, objection to these questions. In his case returns on a few of the children in his unit were in fact sent, though too late for inclusion in the analysis. When this unit head originally received the survey he rang the National Children's Bureau to say that it would be impossible to answer 'yes' to the opinion questions on 'could the child be safely accommodated elsewhere?' because the unit would then be acting unlawfully in holding the child. He referred to the Department of

Health guidance on this point, and argued that the following passage meant if a child could be accommodated in open conditions, **even if the placement did not actually exist,** the child should not be locked up:

> ... restricting the liberty of children in a serious step which must be taken only when there is no appropriate alternative. It must be a 'last resort' in the sense that all else must first have been comprehensively considered and rejected – never because no other placement was available at the relevant time, because of inadequacies in staffing, because the child is simply being a nuisance or runs away from his accommodation and is not likely to suffer significant harm in doing so, and never as a form of punishment.[5]

He therefore wrote on his form: 'Opinion questions have not been answered – since any but one answer to them is self-incriminating their total lack of validity/reliability renders them futile.'

This extremely rigorous interpretation of the Departmental guidance seems admirable but difficult to apply in the case of children who are clearly extremely dangerous but for whom some hypothetical alternative placement would be appropriate. It was made clear in the covering letter that we were not asking the unit heads to criticise social work practice or the courts' judgement, but rather to speculate about what might be – ought to be – provided for these children.

It is possible that a few other managers completing the form felt that an affirmative answer to the opinion questions might in some way be self-incriminating or negate the value of their work. But in any event the majority found no difficulty in responding to these questions.

Out of the 193 children, the managers considered that 60 children (31%) could be safely accommodated in open accommodation (59 of the 60 were considered safe on 31 March, the one remaining was considered safe on admission but not on 31 March). Few considered alternatives were appropriate for the Regulation 6 children, so this proportion is even higher for the Section 25s and 53s:

	Section 25s	Remands	Section 53s
Safe to place in unlocked accommodation on admission	9	2	0
Safe to place in unlocked accommodation on 31 March 1994	34	4	21

The number of affirmative answers to these questions is astonishingly large. It should be remembered that these answers were given at a time when the Criminal Justice and Public Order Act 1994, introducing secure training centres and privatisation of secure accommodation, was passing through Parliament. The media and Parliamentary debates were full of references to the insufficiency of secure unit places and how more places were required as a matter of urgency. It should also be noted that these answers are given by professionals who strongly believe in the value of secure units. Finally it must be remembered that although the child might have been deemed safe to let out it does not necessarily follow that they should have been, since in many cases the safe alternative placement unfortunately did not exist.

Where could the children have been accommodated?

As regards **where** the young people might be safely accommodated, the replies were as follows:

Number of children	Where the children could have been accommodated
3	Back at home
2	Back at home with support
4	In a therapeutic community (two specified that it should have high levels of supervision)
3	In foster care
2	In a psychiatric unit (one specified 'secure')
10	In a children's home (a number said things like 'small', 'good', 'supportive', 'well supervised with secure boundaries')
2	In the open part of a secure unit
3	At a residential school, special school or CHE
5	In supported independent living or lodgings
2	In bail hostels

continued

Number of children	Where the children could have been accommodated
2	In a placement preparing them for reintegration home
3	At a placement with therapy for their needs (two for offending behaviour, one for experiencing sexual abuse)
2	Were due to be discharged shortly
4	Other: 'A small unit with drugs counselling away from home', 'but issue of how to manage this boy's behaviour which appears to be "designed" to raise anxieties of those caring for him', 'a special unit is being set up to accommodated this young person (pathological arsonist) staffed on a 24-hour basis'
3	More than one of the above
10	Not specified

(A number of these responses added the rider 'a long way away from the child's home'. It seems that in some cases integration of children back into their families or communities was a lost cause – better to start afresh).

Which children could have been let out?

What were the behaviours that had caused the locking up of these young people in the first place?

As regards the Section 25 children, of those identified as being held under the absconding ground and self injury ground:

Significant harm risked	Safe to place in unlocked accommodation on admission	Safe to place in unlocked accommodation on 31 March 1994
Solvent abuse/driving	1	5
Solvent abuse		4
Solvent abuse/criminal activities		3
Moral danger/solvent abuse		1
Prostitution female		1
Solvent abuse/self harm		1
Moral danger	1	2
Dangerous driving	1	2
Attempted suicide	2	3
Driving/criminal activities		1
Prostitution male	2	2
Self harm		2
More than one of the above	1	3
Not specified		2

Of the 41 children deemed likely to injure others (of which most were also likely to injure themselves) those with the following behaviours were considered safe to let out:

Injury to others	Safe to place in unlocked accommodation on admission	Safe to place in unlocked accommodation on 31 March 1994
Dangerous driving	3	6
Physical assault		3
Sexual assault	1	3
Arson	1	2
More than one of above		1
Not known		1

As regards the four Regulation 6 remanded children deemed safe to let out:

Grounds and behaviour	Safe to place in unlocked accommodation on admission	Safe to place in unlocked accommodation on 31 March 1994
Absconding	1	2
Charged with violent offence	1	1
Charged with arson *and* self injuring		1

As regards the Section 53 children, the children whom the managers thought could be (though not necessarily should be) safely let out had committed the following offences:

Offence committed	Safe to place in unlocked accommodation on 31 March 94 (No children were identified as being safe to let out on admission)
Robbery	7
Arson	2
Aggravated burglary	2
Manslaughter	1
Rape	2
Attempted rape	1
Kidnapping	1
Robbery and wounding	2
Robbery and burglary	1
Not known	2

It should be noted that more or less the full range of dangerous and self-injuring behaviours identified as making a child eligible for locking up are included in this list, save for the five children who had been convicted of murder (one also convicted of other offences). It seems that, aside from this, there are no behaviours which, even on a randomly selected day, the managers consider axiomatically meant that the child would not be safe to let out. It may also be that the wording of the questionnaire may have caused managers to state that some of those children who had murdered could not be safely let out, not because of risk to public safety but because of risk to the child's own safety from acts of vengeance.

Changing behaviour

In addition the question was asked, of Section 25s and Regulation 6 children: 'Have the grounds changed since admission? If yes, how?' This question was asked in order to discover, for example, if children had acquired new grounds since being admitted to the unit, for example becoming violent or self-injuring. But in the event, for the 15 children (13 Section 25 children and two Regulation 6 children) about whom it was said the grounds had changed, none was to do with worsening behaviour:

No of children	How grounds had changed
7	Said to have shown greater stability, insight or commitment (one made reference to the child winning a youth award scheme).
2	Further information had been obtained (one 'lied about his age', one disclosed more details of abuse)
3	Ceased to display the behaviour, either for a period of time or on mobility (that is, being let out on trial)
1	Had the charges dropped
1	(On remand) had been sentenced to a non-custodial three year supervision order and was being held in the unit under an interim care order
1	Not specified

4. Discussion of behaviours for which children are locked up

Self harming behaviour
Self-injury

Suicidal children are commonly treated in adolescent psychiatric units. If suicide attempts are feared, they may have to be 'specialed' – that is, put under 24-hour personal supervision. Many of the self-injuring children in this survey seemed more obvious candidates for psychiatric interventions. The crude question must be asked: why are the children who head-bang, arm-cut, overdose, drug-abuse or who seek sexual exploitation, in a secure unit and not under some form of health care? Although these are not symptoms of classic forms of mental illness they are behaviour disorders which are also currently treated within adolescent psychiatric units.

Though the discussion group thought that such children often could be treated within open provision, with one-to-one staffing over crisis periods, one group member pointed out:

> ... some young people view the close supervision given in an open setting when there is a need for protection, as more intrusive than secure accommodation. I have come across a number of situations where young people have said that what secure accommodation provides is personal space and privacy inside a secure perimeter as opposed to the feeling of being watched and under surveillance when in an open setting. This is not particularly a defence of secure accommodation as this view is not reflected by other young people and it may be that there is an element of choice or preferred treatment in these situations.

The group agreed with this comment, but acknowledged that young people almost never did get a choice of preferred treatment: they got what the lottery of place and circumstance dealt them.

The discussion group were unusually bitter about the role psychiatrists and mental health services played in relation to secure units. Aside from their unhelpfulness over violent children (see below) the group expressed the general feeling that psychiatric units were spoilt and self-indulgent, taking only adolescents who actively wanted to be treated and tending to take middle class children with eating disorders rather than working class children with multiple problems. The local consultant psychiatrist could wield great influence over the treatment of adolescents in an area; sometimes their personal idiosyncrasies appeared to distort professional judgements. One unit manager described relations between the unit staff and the psychiatric team as being so bad that any meeting between them always resembled a battle ground.

The overriding feeling of the group was that of disappointment, of being let down by the mental health services. However one unit had taken what it regarded as a successful initiative in buying from a local health trust the full time services of a psychologist. Her primary function was to assist the staff in the assessment of children and the development of treatment plans (had her services been to the children directly the health authority would have been responsible for her salary but through this employment device she was paid by the unit but retained the professional support and supervision of the Trust). The group thought that this approach might be the best most cost-efficient use of psychiatrists' and psychologists' expertise.

The units were dealing with young people who, above all, needed treatment. Where the self-injurers were concerned, there was no other point in locking them up except to give them treatment (though treatability is not, as it is in some Mental Health legislation, relevant to detention in secure accommodation). Very few adolescents suffer from classic forms of mental illness: the vast majority appear to suffer from conduct disorders. Recent studies have shown that children are frequently admitted to psychiatric units for social misbehaviour,such as truanting, substance abuse, theft, verbal and physical abuse and running away.[6] A Children's Society survey of units showed children being admitted because of other family members' stressed behaviour, because of homelessness and in order to explore possible sexual abuse.[7] In other words, so far as the self-injurers were concerned, there appears to be a large degree of overlap between psychiatric and secure units with little coherence about the distribution.

Absconding

Self-injury cannot be disentangled from absconding. There was only one self-injuring child who was not a runaway. Otherwise the survey showed that 82% of children in care in the units were deemed to be absconders, as were 40% of the Regulation 6 children.

Running away is a, if not the, behaviour most likely to trigger a secure placement. This is hardly surprising – indeed the question could be asked, if the child does not run away why is it necessary to lock up him or her? On the other hand why should the fact of running away be a specified ground for locking up the child (rather than behaviour cited to justify the ground), **additional** to the grounds of likely to injure self or likely to injure others if not locked up?

Under Section 25 a 'history of absconding' has to be shown; under Regulation 6 this requirement is modified, the court only has to be satisfied that the child is 'likely to abscond' from open accommodation. 'History of absconding' is undefined in law, and no ready working definition emerged from the survey.

'Absconding' itself is unclear – does this only mean absconding from local authority accommodation or does it include running away from home? Does it mean staying out for a significant period, perhaps for 24 hours or overnight, or would (as the discussion group had experienced) a trip out without leave or failing to come back at the appointed hour constitute absconding? The discussion group pointed out that many children have led such chaotic lives that expecting them to respond to strict time-keeping is unrealistic. The group thought that the whole business of recording abscondings could be overly-bureaucratic, just a means for social workers or residential care workers to protect their own backs but not something which translates into attempts to find the child or to discover what is wrong.

The authorities also had to be satisfied that the absconders had a 'history of absconding'. The units were asked 'What was the history of absconding?' The answers were not very illuminating. Most (55%) referred to an unspecified 'persistence' in running away, a few were more specific either about the periods the child had gone for ('days at a time','missing approx three weeks, before that almost daily for short periods') or over what period the abscondings had occurred ('abscondings over a year', 'abscondings over 6-9 months') or both: 'history going back to autumn 1992 slowly and steadily increasing to point when not in placement for more than a few minutes or a few hours overnight occasionally'(in relation to a male prostitute). Certainly there is no perceived definition of a 'history of absconding': the responses included: 'comes from a travellers' family' and 'running back to previous placement where they could not contain her', 'absconding to her father with whom contact is prohibited'.

The absconding ground also includes the condition that the child must be likely to abscond from any other description of accommodation (other than that which restricts liberty). In practice less than a third of the absconding children in the survey appeared to have experienced more than one **type** of accommodation (though many more had run through a number of one type, such as children's homes or foster care). In some cases the respondent made clear that experimenting with open accommodation was out of the question because no one was prepared to take the children on, given their previous history.

As studies have pointed out since the early 1970s, absconding can have more to do with the open placement (with some having consistently higher levels of runaways than others) or with a habit or phase the child is going through, than with any profound disturbance in the child.[8]

As well as having a history of absconding and being likely to abscond from any other provision, the criteria also require that the children are likely to suffer significant harm if they abscond. Running away is what Americans call a 'status offence', an offence which can only be committed by people of a particular status such as soldiers, prisoners, sectioned mental patients or children. The mere fact of running away is sufficient to put children at risk of significant harm in terms of the Children Act definition (see page 7) since their 'normal' emotional and educational development is threatened and they may have to resort to unlawful activities in order to survive. So the criterion starts to be a circular one: runaways are at risk because they run away.

The discussion group recognised that there was a difficulty in determining when the absconding criteria ceased to apply. Some factors, like the relationships the children had with their families or peer groups, were relevant indicators but the only real way to prove that children would not run away again was to test them by letting them out 'on mobility'. Yet if they ran, they might be running away just because they did not like the unit, on the other hand if they did not run it might only be because the secure unit (at no little expense) met their needs in the way open provision could not, or could not afford. The managers did not feel that the Department of Health had given them helpful guidance in the risk-taking involved in letting out absconders, though the Social Services Inspectorate have made clear that they have responsibility for such judgements.

If the absconding criterion was eliminated from Section 25 would it make any difference to the numbers locked up? One could argue that it would not, as the same list of behaviours used to justify 'significant harm' could equally apply to the 'likely to injure self' criterion. But injuring self suggests a stricter test than harm – for example the likelihood of committing offences on the run would surely not constitute self-injury.

Perhaps if absconding was no longer expressly indicated as a reason for locking up children, care authorities might adopt a more imaginative, or relaxed, approach to their runaway children. For example, some countries – such as Denmark – have adopted the strategy of giving runaway children lists of safe addresses where they can stay without being detained. The children are thus able gradually to bring some control into their lives and seek help on their own terms. The Children's Society is developing a similar initiative in this country. The Children Act 'refuges' – safe houses for runaways, like that run by Centrepoint – are a welcome development, although hindered by the 14-day time-limit on placements.

Prostitution and moral danger

It was sometimes difficult to discern which of the children were locked up because they were embarking on a career of prostitution and which were being locked up because they were at risk of being sexually exploited or abused. Risk of sexual abuse has been termed here as 'moral danger' because it is probable the children themselves would not agree they were being abused and were in some way actively colluding or seeking the sexual contact, hence the locked placement. This is sometimes stated explicitly: 'associating with adult males with Schedule 1 status and known to seek out males with a sexual history involving boys and males with pornographic material', 'Actually suffered not a little moral danger and some physical problems regarding a sexually transmitted disease which she contracted… This girl is generally viewed as being immature and naive and certainly at risk of being manipulated sexually', 'Association with 35-year-old man'. Where it was possible the children who were engaged in prostitution have been distinguished but there may be more in this category when vague terms such as 'sexual risk' have been used.

The discussion group saw these children as particularly difficult if not impossible to treat, not least because the criteria for placement disappeared as soon as they were locked up. The male and female prostitutes were often indignant about the placement, regarding themselves as following a lucrative profession which adults also pursued. Some girls would admit to enjoying having a respite from the job and getting the health clean-ups and health education the unit offered, but this did not prevent them from going back to prostitution as soon as they were let out.

There was also a strikingly counter-productive side to locking these children up, which was that, when this matter was being discussed, every group member present at the meeting said that he or she could think of cases where children who were not prostitutes in the unit had been recruited – either by children already acting as prostitutes or by their pimps. (Indeed this was given in the survey as one reason for the secure unit placement – 'recruited girls in children's home into prostitution'. From what the discussion group said this child may well have continued this activity in the secure unit, with perhaps even easier converts).

The primary reason for locking up such children was seen as political: that if they were not locked up social services risked being pilloried in the media. This was not to say that such children were not being damaged by the experiences or were not themselves very damaged individuals. Many of them had been sexually abused as children, had no self-esteem and were unable to form relationships; as can been seen in the above statistics many combined moral danger with other forms of self-harm such as substance abuse or self-mutilation. But the discussion group thought that the most effective response was to tackle it on the streets – one mentioned a successful project which enlisted the adult prostitutes in policing child prostitution (though there are obvious risks in such an approach as most child prostitutes are introduced into the 'game' by adult prostitutes in the first place). Another approach would be to set up small flexible open units in the locality where the children would be encouraged to form relationships with people who were not involved in prostitution and to offer alternatives to this trade.

Substance abuse

The discussion group members commented that, of the wide range of children they are dealing with, those on drugs are the ones most likely to **ask** to be locked up – sometimes because they want to come off drugs, sometimes because they want protection from drug dealers (two of the children in the survey fell into the latter category). However, as with prostitution, the group members did not feel that units were as effective a form of intervention as open specialist drug rehabilitation services or street-based services.

The reasons why the children were locked up were either political, in that the care authority could not risk the consequences, not to the child but to itself, of not locking the child up or because of the other anti-social behaviour connected with the substance abuse – stealing or dangerous driving.

Behaviour harming others

Dangerous driving

A main reason for locking up the Section 25 and Regulation 6 children was that their habit of stealing cars made them a danger to themselves and others. The large numbers are not surprising. March 1994 followed a long media outcry against 'TWOCers' and crazed teenagers doing hand-brake turns in council estates, not to mention young 'joyriders' killing themselves and other people. Undoubtedly unlicensed children driving cars which do not belong to them for kicks are potentially very dangerous.

One difficulty is the scale of the problem. A unit manager pointed out that in the last year in his area alone there had been 1,236 arrests of young people for taking and driving cars. They were all potentially dangerous but could not all be locked up. The group thought that persistence was relevant but only in terms of showing likelihood of doing it again: 'persistence' was a popular term with the Government but a highly subjective one – it could mean three offences or three hundred, or lots of offences over a short period or less over longer. One manager speculated that the majority of children in the unit because of car crime were already in care before the offence – in other words the local authority felt more obliged to lock up dangerous driving children in children's homes than children who were previously living with their parents. The other group members agreed that this theory was likely, but there was no means of testing it through the survey returns.

Seriousness of the circumstances seemed to the group to be the more relevant factor – careering around an estate at 80 miles an hour, or driving the wrong way down a motor way, or driving when drunk or under the influence of solvents. It was agreed that the way forward was in motor projects and other projects which recognised the need these children had for thrills – whether from bungee jumping or from fast cars – as well as the need to educate them about the consequences of their actions. Although motor projects do not always succeed in diverting children from their addiction to stealing cars (the National Association of Motor Projects claims a seven out of ten success rate) it is appears that locking up children has no deterrent effect: a local study suggested that the re-offending rate for young offenders sentenced to custody for car-related offences is nearly 100%.[9] Making cars more difficult to steal – locks, security cameras and so on – was another obvious preventive approach.

Remanded children

Children who are remanded to secure units are in a curious position. Seventeen-year-olds are treated as adult offenders and are not remanded to local authority accommodation. As regards 16-year-olds and under, once charged with an offence then they will be remanded to local authority accommodation if they are refused bail for reasons equivalent to an adult offender, including:

That the court believed the young person would:

- fail to come to court when required;
- commit an offence on bail;
- interfere with witnesses or obstruct justice.

or where the young person has already breached bail or bail conditions, where the young person has to be held while more information is gathered or because the court believes that refusal of bail would be for the young person's welfare.

Having failed to achieve bail (with or without conditions) the child is remanded 'to local authority accommodation'. Before the Children Act this was a remand to care: the change of terminology reflects the fact that the local authority does not owe the child the same parenting duties it does to a child in care.

Once the child is remanded, the authority can then apply to court for a secure placement under Section 25 or Regulation 6 (see above). It is perhaps curious that these criteria do not correspond to the refusal of bail criteria. For example, as regards the likelihood of absconding, it could be argued that there is a big difference between running away to avoid a court hearing and running back home from a children's home. (The survey therefore asked: 'was the absconding likely to mean that the young person would not attend court for trial or sentencing?'; for at least one out of the 35 it was said it did not). And although some children were being locked up because it was feared they would otherwise pervert the course of justice this is not actually a ground for a secure accommodation place. Tampering with evidence, for example, might not injure anyone.

Since implementation of the Criminal Justice Act 1991 under transitional arrangements 15 and 16-year-old boys can be remanded by the youth court to prison. When the Act is fully implemented the court will be able to impose a 'security requirement' to order local authorities to place in secure accommodation 15 and 16-year-olds who meet the Regulation 6 offending or absconding conditions (see page 11). The grounds justifying such a requirement then differ from Regulation 6, the court having only to be:

of the opinion that only such a requirement would be adequate to protect the public from serious harm from him.

Under 1994 Criminal Justice and Public Order Act provisions, the power to impose a security requirement is extended to 12 to 14-year-olds (to be implemented in phased stages), to allow for the locking up of children destined for the new secure training centres.

The 1994 Act also enables the Secretary of State to reimburse local authorities for the cost of a court secure requirement. She undertook to meet 'the fair cost of secure accommodation' but it is now understood that the Home Office is to take responsibility for this funding. It is hard not to believe that this provision, reasonable though it is, will not act as an incentive to the authority to encourage a security requirement – thus avoiding both the cost and responsibility for accommodating remanded children in open provisions.

Not, indeed, that many courts appear to need incentives to lock up children; the difficulty is rather to fetter their powers so that only the necessary minimum are locked up. Following implementation of the 1991 Act there was a sharp increase in the numbers of 15 and 16-year-old boys remanded to prison, with no notable reduction of those charged with non-dangerous property-related offences. A report by NACRO and the Association of Chief Officers of Probation also revealed dramatic geographical variations in such remands, with disproportionately more in the north of England than the south.[10]

The report pointed out that in some areas few or no children were locked up on remand, whether to prison or secure accommodation. This appeared to relate to the extent of bail information and bail support schemes. A Home Office consultation on remand provisions in the 1991 Act stated:

When the proposals in this paper are fully implemented, the Government expects the number of juveniles remanded with a security condition to be considerably lower than the number remanded in prison department custody. The Government also hopes that the development of alternative diversionary arrangements will encourage a reduction in the number of such

remands. For example, as courts' confidence in bail support
schemes develops, it is expected that a greater proportion of juve-
niles will be granted bail.

But until bail support schemes are mandatory it seems likely that
these hopes will remain unfulfilled.

Children on remand are a markedly different group to the others in secure units. They are likely to fall into two categories: those
who are being locked up because they have been charged with very
serious offences and those who have committed relatively petty
offences (car theft, burglary) to an unacceptably persistent or dangerous degree.

Both groups are likely to have social and emotional problems.
For example the recent study by the Policy Studies Institute
revealed 'overwhelmingly chaotic' histories of family and educational disruption in the most persistent offenders they encoun-
tered.[11]

Nonetheless for the most part remanded children have not been
convicted of their alleged offences and are technically innocent.
Their stay in the unit can be a long one – of the survey's Section
53 group, one child had spent 11 months in the unit before sentencing, one ten months and three nine months; five of the 35
Regulation 6 children had spent more than 70 days at the unit.
But, because of their status, offence-related rehabilitative work
could not be undertaken during this period lest it interfere with
the course of justice.

The discussion group agreed that remanded children were
therefore different from the rest of the secure unit population.
They also said that sometimes remanded children could have an
adverse effect on the rest of the group. It was likely that the future
increase in remands could significantly change the nature of
secure units, distorting their rehabilitative approach.

The UN Rules for the Protection of Juveniles Deprived of their
Liberty requires that: 'untried juveniles should be separated from
convicted juveniles'. The discussion group considered that there
was a logic in having separate units for remanded children, but
members were concerned about the possible unintended consequences of such a change. Firstly such units would have to be run
on a welfare, not penal, basis. Although offence-related work could
not be done many other of the children's difficulties could be tack-
led. If, for example, the private sector was used, the likelihood was
that the units would just become warehouses. One alternative
possibility was that special remand units could function as assessment centre which could assist the courts in identifying which

children needed to be locked up on sentencing. However concern was expressed that this might lead to more children being locked up, or for longer periods than an adult of an equivalent charge. Nonetheless the group thought that the potential of special remand centres should be explored.

Persistent property-related offending

The population of secure units is not intended to include children who are persistent but relatively petty offenders. Nonetheless it was clear that some of the Section 25 children had been locked up on the grounds that they were absconders who were risking 'significant harm' because their 'emotional, social or behavioural development' was being threatened by criminal offending. This would be most likely for the ten to 14 age-group, below the age eligible for a young offender institution sentence. The units also accommodate young people remanded on charges of property-related offences.

Secure training centres for 12 to 14-year-old petty offenders, introduced to much public controversy in the 1994 Criminal Justice and Public Order Act, were supposed to cover a gap in legislation whereby the 'One-Boy Crime Wave', 'Ratboy', 'Sutton Posse' and so forth were able to pursue their criminal activities without check. Throughout the previous year the papers and politicians cited a number of cases where children (not necessarily under 15) had racked up dozens of arrests and convictions, sometimes committing more than a thousand offences in all. Most included dangerous activities – car-theft, robbery, assault – but a few appeared to have limited their careers to theft and burglary.

Should such children be locked up? The first point to be made is that, contrary to allegation, some of the notorious cases **had** been locked up in secure accommodation under Section 25 conditions and had then continued to offend as merrily as before. Locking them up worked neither as a deterrent nor a cure.

However their period inside may simply have been a welcome respite for the communities they had been preying upon. If nothing else, Government spokespersons have argued, lock-ups can be justified for taking these children off the streets. But there are big risks. The Government has been rightly criticised for substituting the word 'trainees' for 'children' in the Secure Training Centre Rules. Trainees is undoubtedly what these children will be: trained by each other in criminal techniques and attitudes. Every lock-up appears to intensify offending. What is more, the as yet unpublished report on the outcomes of Lisneven, the Northern

Ireland juvenile prison, has found not only high levels of offending but more serious offending by ex-inmates: three years after release 86% of the 592 inmates had reoffended, rising to 95% thereafter with the 6% of violent offenders rising to 20%.[12]

Section 53s and seriously dangerous children

The discussion group was not surprised to learn that over a third of the Section 53 children in the survey were considered safe to let out. Many had personal experience of children who, though convicted of grave crimes, were no threat to anyone. One member described a Section 53 boy who had been sent to his unit after spending months out on bail, during which he had got an apprenticeship and was starting to make a go of things. At least one of Section 53 children in the survey had his request for release, supported by the secure unit, turned down by the Home Secretary. In both these cases factors other than public safety determined the outcome.

Current procedures charge the Home Secretary with determining the period in which a child is locked up the under Section 53 sentence (and in the case of murder, the length of the sentence itself). Factors which he takes into account are public safety, the need to maintain public confidence in the system of justice and the requirements of retribution and deterrence. The judiciary have similar considerations when passing custodial sentences. Every child sentenced under Section 53 will have a 'sentence care plan', reviewed at three monthly intervals, to which the secure unit staff contribute alongside relevant others (such as the child's social services) and which will inform the Home Secretary's decisions on placement.

The group also raised the fact that some children convicted of grave offences were released despite the unit staff being sure they would offend again (and subsequently having this belief confirmed). Pathological behaviour such as sexual offending and arson were particularly susceptible to this sort of prediction, though no assessment of probable dangerousness was perfect. Currently staff in secure units were struggling with risk assessment. They did not find specialist psychiatric advice very helpful: two group members described seeking psychiatric assessments which resulted in a diagnosis along the lines of: 'This child is dangerously violent and must be kept locked up for the foreseeable future, but there is no mental illness present and we therefore cannot assist.' The group considered that there seemed to be a general reluctance of psychiatric units to take on violent children.

Some risk-assessment checklists or models were of use, group members said, but could be made more useful – for example patterns of previous offending are crucially important but often children's care histories omit, down-play or disguise earlier offending for fear of labelling them (or sometimes for fear of the resources which are implied in such labelling). The secure units and youth treatment centres have now dealt with large numbers of very dangerous children and efforts should be put into pooling and evaluating these experiences.

The group agreed that there were real problems about relying on dangerousness as the primary criterion for locking up and releasing children, but the group was also attracted to the idea. Even though some children were clearly dangerous, society could not simply lock them up and throw away the key: psychiatrists should not be given control over this civil liberties issue any more than politicians. Some members also thought that the public's and the victim's desire for punishment would always have to be satisfied to some degree. Nevertheless the primary objective should be the restoration of the young offender to a viable non-offending life in the community. The recent transfer of responsibility for seeking and financing secure unit placements for children sentenced under Section 53 from the Department of Health to the Home Office gives no confidence that this is the aim of the Government.[13]

One obvious flaw to risk assessment in units was that the child was behaving in an artificial environment, and children on long-term placements could be profoundly institutionalised. Much more effort had to be put into the transition period after release, when the children were particularly vulnerable to reverting to earlier habits and lifestyles.

Finally, studies in the 1970s showed that a significant proportion of violent assaults, triggering a secure placement, were directed solely at staff members in previous residential placements, with some strong indications that the assault had been provoked by the home or school staff, or by its regime.[14] Once a child has been violent to residential staff he or she of course becomes much harder to place, particularly in small relaxed homes with liberal regimes. The child is therefore trapped in a spiral downwards through stricter placements more likely to alienate and provoke. The problem is as much to do with the care system as with the child. What is needed are improvements to residential care – better resourcing and better staff training, particularly in managing and defusing aggression.

5. Uneven or discriminatory distribution

Geographical

A Department of Health-commissioned research into the use of secure accommodation in the 1980s concluded:

> *the most potent predictor of the high usage of secure accommodation is a local authority's possession of a secure unit.*[15]

The survey showed that the 131 children either looked after by local authorities or remanded to local authority accommodation on 31 March 1994 were the responsibility of the following authorities:

Numbers of children	Local authority
11	Birmingham (9 Section 25, 2 Reg 6)
10	Avon (9 Section 25, 2 Reg 6)
5	Nottinghamshire
4	Hampshire, Oxfordshire, Devon, Lancashire, Humberside
3	Somerset, Newham
2	Bedfordshire, Berkshire, Bradford, Cambridgeshire, Croydon, Doncaster, Dorset, Durham, Gwynedd, Oldham, Stockport, Sunderland, Lincolnshire, Leeds, North Yorkshire
1	Barnsley, Bexley, Bolton, Brent, Buckinghamshire, Calderdale, Cornwall,Cleveland, Cheshire, Coventry, Derbyshire, Dyfed, East Sussex, Enfield, Gloucestershire, Gwent, Hackney, Harrow, Kent, Leicestershire, Lewisham, Liverpool, Manchester, Mid-Glamorgan, Newcastle, North Tyneside, Northamptonshire, Northumberland, Salford, Shropshire, South Tyneside, Southwark, Staffordshire, Suffolk, Surrey, Tower Hamlets, Wakefield, West Sussex, Wiltshire, Wolverhampton, Cumbria, Norfolk
7	Not specified

Eight of the top ten authorities in this list (those placing over two children) own and manage their own secure units.

Three arguments could be made against drawing the conclusion that the high users of secure accommodation tend to be those who manage units. Firstly the survey only gives a snapshot picture of one day which perhaps only reflects a crisis point in the authority's care system, secondly some of the authorities at the top of the list have very large populations which explains their high usage and thirdly some authorities which manage their own units do not use them very much.

The Departmental statistics can throw more light on the first two arguments. In a table showing the number and rate of new admissions per 10,000 children aged 10-17 during the year ending March 31 1994 the top authorities were:

Authority	Rate per 10,000	Number
Hammersmith	10.2	10
Lambeth	7.9	16
Tower Hamlets	6.5	12
Southwark	5.9	11
Kensington	5.8	5
Hackney	5.7	10
Humberside	5.3	46
Haringey	5.7	10
Coventry	5.1	42
Sunderland	4.9	15
Gateshead	4.8	9
Ealing	4.2	11
Birmingham	4.1	42

Here the correlation between managing and using is lower – only five authorities (Hammersmith, Southwark, Humberside, Coventry and Birmingham) manage their own units and the list is otherwise dominated by small London Boroughs. (It should be noted that the length of placement appears to be lower in the South, so, although there may be more admissions it does not follow that there are more locked places).

It is true that some authorities which manage units do not have high rates of placements in secure accommodation. For example only one St Helens child was locked up in 1993-4 (0.5 per 10,000); Liverpool only locked up 4 (0.9% – dropping from 8.7% in 1991) and Salford also locked up 4 (1.9% – again dropping from 5.2% in

1990). These are managing authorities achieving some of the lowest rates in the country.

From the observations of the discussion group it seems likely that a deliberate effort has been made by some authorities to distance themselves from the units they manage – setting them up as self-sufficient financial units, so that the managing authority does not subsidise and has neither the advantage of cheaper places nor priority on beds.

By contrast it appeared that a number of managing authorities do still expect priority treatment, for example by reserving beds – some units even make explicit reference to this in their statements of purpose. Certainly it still remains true that if you are a child living in an authority which runs a secure unit you are by and large more likely to end up in one. (What happens to children who might be eligible for a secure place but are not locked up is as yet unresearched, save that there is little statistical evidence to suggest that they end up in prison).

Another factor also greatly increases your chances of being locked up: media coverage. As can be seen from the above figures Birmingham had locked up 11 children on the survey day and was also near the top of the league for admissions during the previous year. Birmingham also had the experience of being singled out for vilification in the press for not having locked up a 15-year-old girl who died driving a stolen car having absconded from the unit's open section on 15 March 1993. The media furore led to a formal request by the Health Minister for Birmingham to review its secure accommodation decision-making. Such pressures undoubtedly affect authorities' willingness to take risks in not locking children up.

Gender

There were more boys than girls in the units, and girls were more likely to be locked up for reasons connected to self-harm than danger to others. Thus as regards the total population, there were 140 males and 52 females (and one Section 53 of unidentified sex), distributed as follows:

Legal status	Males	Females
Section 25s	62	34
Remands	26	9
Section23s	52	9

Where the absconding ground was cited the difference between the groups is marked. The behaviours identified under the 'risk of significant harm' can be divided between those that are potentially dangerous to others as well as the child and those that are only dangerous to the child:

Gender	Self-harming behaviour also likely to injure others (dangerous driving and criminal activities)	Self-harming behaviour (Substance abuse, moral danger / prostitution, self-harm, attempted suicide)
Boys	25	10
Girls	2	25

(Nine of the 25 self-injuring girls were deemed in moral danger.)

Where the ground 'likely to injury to other persons' was cited:

Gender	Behaviour likely to injure others
Boys	30
Girls	11 (seven having a history of physical assault and two of arson, the rest unspecified).

Of the nine girls who were sentenced under Section 53:

Female grave offenders	Offence
2	Robbery
2	Arson
2	Murder
1	Grievous bodily harm
1	Attempted robbery
1	False imprisonment

(Two were thought safe to let out, both convicted of robbery.)

A recent unpublished analysis by the Social Services Inspectorate points out that, from the statistical returns, over the nine years the proportion of girls in secure units has fluctuated between 52% and 29% and varies between authorities from 0.22 in one authority to 22.00 per 10,000 in another; that girls tend to be admitted younger and readmitted more often than boys.

One Inspector suggested that there was a difference between

seriously distressed and disturbed young women 'for whom secure units provide a "sanctuary" often for extended periods as they begin to disclose and work on and hopefully come to terms with the past' and those 'perhaps larger number who chose or drift into what are seen as unacceptable lifestyles particularly viz sexual partners, drug abuse etc. With this group it is arguable whether a period in a secure unit, which we know is likely to be a short one, is really going to make a difference.'

This seems a reasonable doubt, but it also seems reasonable to wonder whether the treatment and sanctuary offered to the group of seriously distressed and disturbed young women could not sometimes have been offered in an unlocked setting. Masud Hoghughi comments on the adverse reaction girls often had to placement in secure units, becoming fiercely violent or self-destructive.[16]

Concern was also expressed by the discussion group about mixing girls with boys within the unit, and about current government policy to encourage only the expansion of mixed units. While the presence of girls was usually good for boys the reverse was not true, particularly as girls are more likely to be in the units for self-harming behaviour, often arising from histories of sexual abuse (one London Borough calculated that over 80% of girls placed in secure accommodation had been abused). It is difficult to see how such girls could benefit from being locked up with convicted rapists and violent offenders. One of the managers commented that he was looking after boys whom he considered should not be let within a mile of a girl.

Ethnicity

The survey also asked about the children's ethnic origin, not revealed by Government statistics. The survey population was as follows:

Ethnic origin	S 25s	Remands	S 53s	Total	%
White	86	26	47	159	82.5
Black Caribbean/African	6	3	10	19	10
Asian	1	3	3	7	3.5
Other	2		1	3	1.5
Not known	1	3	1	5	2.5

The number of black children of Caribbean/African origin in the units is significantly above the English/Welsh proportions for the age groups, which in 1991 was just below 3%. As interesting, the Asian proportion is below the English/Welsh proportion (around 5%).

These figures correspond with other indications of disproportionate treatment of Caribbean/African origin children, for example that in some areas their numbers in care is above the norm, and figures also show that this group is over-represented in Young Offender Institutions.

The greatest disproportion in the survey came within the Section 53s (16% of that group) reflecting either greater offending (arguably as much linked to their class or their location in inner-cities) or discriminatory sentencing for these black children. For the six under Section 25, the behaviours were:

Black Caribbean / African children	Cited behaviours
2	Female prostitution
1	Drugs and crime
1	Attempted suicide
2	Criminal behaviour
1	Recruited others to prostitution

As so often with these indications of disproportionate treatment, more research is needed to discover the implications. For example it would be interesting to know the proportions of African/Caribbean children in alternative, less punitive provision – for example their preponderance in adolescent psychiatric units as well as in the penal system. Equally useful studies could be made on why Asian children are under-represented in the units.

6. Future management and provision of secure units

Expansion by government

The number of approved places in secure accommodation currently available is 290. The Government plans to fund an additional 170 places by 1995-1996. This expansion has been deemed necessary for the following reasons:

- 100 places are for the 15 and 16-year-old boys who are currently remanded to prison or remand centres under an 'unruly certificate'. Section 60 of the Criminal Justice Act 1991 will, when implemented, repeal the power to remand in penal custody and replace it with a 'security requirement' enabling the court to order a young person in similar circumstances to be placed in secure accommodation. This figure of 100 was initially projected as 65, following Departmental consultations with relevant bodies in 1991-2, but had to be revised upward to 100 because the numbers of penal remands, which had steadily diminished throughout the late 1980s, rose after implementation of the 1991 Act (coinciding with a major media scare about juvenile crime and 'bail bandits').

- 60 places are deemed necessary to meet the new court powers in the 1994 Criminal Justice and Public Order Act to remand 12 to 14-year-olds. The figure is based on Home Office calculations about the use of the new Secure Training Centres for this age-group. The assumption is that if they need to be locked up after sentence then they should also be locked up on remand.

- Ten places were calculated as necessary to receive the ten to 13-year-old children convicted under Section 53(2) of the 1933 Act when this provision of the 1994 Act comes into force. The forecast was that about 40 children would receive this sentence, but that there would be a likely parallel decrease of 30 15 and 16-year-olds receiving short Section 53(2) sentences –

instead they would be sentenced under the longer young offender institution sentences available under the 1993 Act.

The proposed expansion of secure units is intended to 'iron out' some of the geographical discrepancies in the use of lock-ups described above, but to some extent this may not be possible. Figures given to the Bureau by the Department show the following expansion:

Region	Places at 31 March 1994	New places	Total
North East	55	7	62
North West	66	23	89
Yorks/Humberside	37	17	54
West Midlands	16	20	36
East Midlands	17	21	38
Thames/Anglia	9	34	43
London	35	16	49
Southern	22	18	32
South West	32	10	42
Wales	0	6	6
Total	289	172	461

Thus the North will have 205 places to 123 in both the Midlands and the South respectively. This discrepancy can in part be explained by the fact that three of the four large regional secure units are located in the North (the two youth treatment centres in the Midlands and the South serving a similar purpose). Nonetheless it appears that the North will have to continue to have more secure places in order to receive the 15 and 16-year-old boys presently remanded to Prison Department custody when the 1991 Criminal Justice Act is fully implemented. For as the NACRO report[10] showed, the Northern regions remanded to prison custody an average of 1.74 boys per 10,000 as opposed to 0.38 in the South in the year April 1992 to March 1993.

Expansion by privatisation

The 1994 Act also 'demonopolises' secure units – throwing open both the management and the ownership of them to the private and voluntary sector. In effect this means privatising the units, since no voluntary organisation has indicated it is interested in running units.

Aside from questions of morality (is it ethically right to make profits from locking up children? Is not the restriction of liberty the proper business of the State?) and aside from questions of quality (can the private sector provide the necessary high standards of care and actually make a profit?) the privatising of secure units raises a real concern that this will increase the numbers of children locked up, while decreasing their capacity to treat and rehabilitate.

This is because the history of secure accommodation shows that the normal rules of supply and demand are reversed, in that demand follows supply. Locked places for difficult teenagers are filled as soon as they become available; if they are not available other alternatives are found.

For example grant-aid in 1985 for the capital cost of secure units was introduced to meet the policy in the 1969 Children and Young Persons Act ending juvenile custody and remands to prison. In 1992 a Department of Health official said:

> *Not surprisingly, many local authorities embraced this largesse with open arms and the late 70s and early 80s saw a rapid expansion of the stock of secure accommodation. Unfortunately, the additional places were rapidly filled with children in local authority care, who, overnight it seemed, suddenly became too difficult to manage in open conditions. You will not be surprised that we are still, even in 1992, talking about the need to plan for the complete abolition of juvenile penal remands and wondering how it is possible to provide more secure accommodation without it being filled with children who do not really need to be there.*[17]

As Harris and Timms point out: there are many children who are potential candidates for secure unit places and 'the existence of more and hence 'easier' secure places may demotivate authorities in their efforts to produce creative alternatives or improve the quality of their open establishments'.[15]

Unlike privatising prison, where the number of prisoners is determined by the judiciary and sentencing policy, private secure accommodation is dependent on a subjective judgement of the child's 'best interests'.

The discussion group was pessimistic about the impact of privatisation. One of the most important, and little-known, points to emerge from the group was that secure unit managers can play an important role in stopping children from being unnecessarily locked up. All the managers in the group had refused to accept children whom they considered did not meet the legal criteria, even if a court order had been obtained. They did not consider that this was outside their remit since, as one pointed out, if the Social Services Inspectorate discovered that they were accommodating children who did not meet the criteria they would undoubtedly lose their licences.

The managers on the group acknowledged that they would also sometimes refuse to accept children who did need to be locked up if they felt these children would destroy the progress and balance of the existing group of children in the unit. In other words they would give priority to the needs of the children they were caring for, rather than those they were not. There are of course limits to this, in that there are strong financial incentives to keep places filled and costs down, but the group strongly believed that some degree of flexibility over intake was essential to meet the needs of the children.

Although this filtering of children by the unit was practised by group members it is not universally the case among secure units. It was reported that a number are currently under great stress because management required they adopt the 'hotel approach' of taking all-comers, regardless of whether they needed to be locked up or whether the unit could meet their needs or the impact they might have on the other children.

In short the group feared that privatising the units would, by creating more places and by not being so choosy about who they took, inevitably lead to many more children being locked up unnecessarily.

Specialisation

The discussion group tended towards the view that units ought to be more specialised, both in terms of gender and particular needs or offences. They were not particularly in favour of age-based specialisation, arguing that the children's chronological ages were often at odds with their emotional or behavioural ages. They recognised that specialised locked units might mean that children were placed further away from their homes. However geographical distance from home was a surmountable problem: what was needed by the placing authority was commitment and resources. Plans should always be made and budgets allocated to ensure that social workers and families visit regularly. Unfortunately this was not always done, even when the child's home was nearby.

Specialisation is not a part of the Government's expansion programme: because special units would be likely to have fluctuating intakes it would be difficult to make them financially viable. However the Government has required that the new units and the expansions of existing units should be 'flexible' so that, for instance, a segregated girls-only living and sleeping section could be provided within a mixed sex, mixed behaviour unit if the need arose.

Attached open provision

The group were convinced of the need for secure units to have open provision, with continuity of staffing and programmes, to which the children could transfer as soon as the need to lock them up disappeared. Without this kind of transition the children sometimes found it impossible to adjust to the demands of a comparatively unstructured and unsupported open placement back in their communities. Moreover it was also less labelling to come to a new permanent place from an open half-way placement than from the more stigmatising locked placement.

The difficulty here was that the cost of the intensive support in the 'open secure unit' was as high, or sometimes higher (because of the need for more staff) than in the locked unit. They found that local authorities were able to bear and justify the high cost of a secure unit place, but would not countenance paying these sums for an unlocked place. One suggestion was that these half-way highly staffed open units could be provided on a regional basis.

The Government's plans to not require attached open provision – it is understood that at least three of the new secure units are 'green field units', standing alone. The Government is not convinced that open provision ensures that children are discharged quicker from the locked unit: on the contrary it is argued that having open and locked units on the same site sometimes leads to abuse, with the locked unit being over-used as a control mechanism.

7. What can be done to limit the numbers locked up?

Alternatives to locking up children

There has been no shortage of proposals for increasing and improving the range and number of community-based alternatives to lock-ups for children. For example NACRO, The Children's Society and NCH-Action for Children have all made practical suggestions for re-allocating resources into preventive and non-custodial facilities. Recommendations include:

- ring-fenced funding for preventive or community-based services for children on remand, young offenders and otherwise behaviourally disturbed children;
- local authority social services to be placed under clear statutory duties to provide or to secure the provision of such services, including:
  - family support schemes;
  - bail support schemes;
  - special foster care schemes for 'difficult adolescents' and those on remand;
  - 'alternative to custody projects';
  - open access and referred family centres;
  - shared care schemes;
  - youth projects;
  - therapeutic communities;
  - a range of residential children's homes with well-trained staff on a good
  - child:staff ratio;
  - specialist community-based projects, with both outreach and residential
  - provision, for substance-abusers and prostitutes (male and female);
  - motor projects;
  - 'absconder' or street schemes safe addresses (provided

without strings for runaway or otherwise homeless children to use at their discretion).

- local education authorities, health authorities and other appropriate agencies to be placed under statutory duties to assist and collaborate with social services in the planning and commissioning of such services and in strategies to reduce destructive and self-destructive behaviour in children;
- models should be explored which encourage greater involvement by those who are most concerned. For example versions of the New Zealand initiative of 'family group conferences' (whereby victim, investigating officer, parents, young offender and social worker attempt to agree the disposal) or of the Danish practice – commended by the Home Affairs Select Committee[1] of allowing young offenders a say in their sentencing, could be piloted.

Many commentators have criticised the failure of central Government to give priority to these alternative services and strategies, preferring in England and Wales (though not Scotland) to put money into locked places – more secure units, new secure training centres, longer young offender institution orders. None of the services listed above are provided consistently across the country and some facilities are actually diminishing, such as residential care, outreach work or therapeutic communities. Although there are a couple of Government schemes to encourage their development (for example the 'supervision grant scheme' at the Home Office, or the Support Force for Children's Residential Care sponsored by the Department of Health) the resources they receive are pitiful in comparison to say, the £30-£100 million being spent on secure training centres.

Legislative reform

The discussion group indicated that, in their view, the limited numbers of secure places, their high cost and the units' own unofficial filtering systems were the most effective factors at present for keeping down the numbers of children unnecessarily locked up. It was suggested that, as the legal criteria could be applied to an excessively large group of children (for example encompassing more or less all absconders, all those who take and drive cars, all those who become involved in substance abuse and so forth) the law could not be solely relied upon as an effective check on unsuitable placements.

This report does not address the court process, and little

research appears to have been done on secure orders in recent years. Anecdotal reports suggest that since the Children Act 1989 introduction of guardians *ad litem*, a rubber-stamping of secure orders has diminished, with more applications being refused by the courts. Nonetheless the legal grounds for Section 25 orders under the 1989 Act and secure requirement orders under the l994 Act do appear very unsatisfactory.

Hard proposals for legal reform cannot be made here: more debate, consultation and thought is needed. But the findings of this report point to some preliminary conclusions about how the grounds might be reformed. These include:

- that children likely to injure themselves should not be locked up unless **either** this is the only way to prevent them from killing themselves or doing themselves permanent physical damage **or** that if kept in any description of open provision they are likely to injure themselves **and** that the self-injuring behaviour can be alleviated or prevented by treatment given within the secure accommodation placement. (Below we suggest that such children should not be accommodated with dangerous children);

- that the absconding ground in Section 25 should be abandoned;

- the Section 25 criterion 'likely to injure others if kept in any other description of accommodation' should remain for unconvicted, remanded and convicted children as the principal ground for restricting their liberty. The court should prescribe maximum periods of detention but, as with Section 25, the child should be released before that date if the criterion no longer applies;

- in addition the local authority should be able to apply for a secure order for remanded children if satisfied that the child is likely to fail to appear at court or is likely to try to pervert the course of justice;

- that the court should consider not just the grounds for admitting a child to secure accommodation but should also be satisfied at the application hearing that plans and facilities exist to secure that the child is discharged in the shortest appropriate time to accommodation suitable to the child's needs.

Central gatekeeping and a national strategy

The proposals for reform of the criteria do not solve all the problems raised by this report. For example, even with these grounds courts and local authorities would still be able to lock up children fairly easily. The geographical variations would not be ironed out. Nor does the reformed legislation address what is to be done with children who are not dangerous but who do commit persistent property-related offences on a publicly unacceptable scale and who have exhausted all community-based alternatives. It can be assumed that the numbers of such children would be radically diminished if resources were diverted into preventive and community-based strategies described above but it could not be assumed that there would be no such children.

Many of the discussion group's criticisms of current secure accommodation procedures led them to the view that what was needed was a national strategy and strong central direction. One commented:

> *I find it quite bizarre that such an expensive and controversial service is managed without a clear overall national strategy and largely at the whim of individual local authorities which change with political climates.*

Not only does this report endorse this view but it also recommends that the concept of **central gatekeeping on individual placements** be pursued. This would not replace local authorities' responsibilities for children in need in their area, and the need to protect the public from some of these children, nor would it replace those children's rights to due process – to have any restriction of liberty examined and tested in a court hearing. What is proposed here is that beyond this there should be a further hurdle to jump before any child could be locked up.

The Home Affairs Select Committee recommended a National Agency on youth justice which would:

> *manage the custody and supervision of persistent juvenile offenders and others who receive custodial sentences. We recommend the agency be funded centrally, and be given wide discretion to manage the young people in its care on an individual basis up to the age of 18, with the intention of stopping the juveniles concerned committing further crimes and helping them by education, vocational training and therapy to live law-abiding adult lives.*[1]

This recommendation has been cautiously welcomed by many working in this field. The Select Committee did not go so far as to suggest that the proposed national agency would have powers to determine the locking up of all children. Its proposals were confined to 15 and 16-year-olds on young offender institution senten-ces and those under supervision residential requirements, they did not apply extend to Section 53 offenders, self-injuring children or those on remand.

It is proposed here that such an Agency could in fact be set up to approve and oversee **all** placements of children in locked accom-modation, charged with the duty to secure that, in line with the UN Convention, children are locked up only as a last resort for the shortest appropriate time. Backed by Government resources it would encourage the establishment of services designed to pre-vent delinquency and custody and would tackle regional varia-tions. In addition the Agency would also approve each individual placement in secure accommodation, the placement having first been approved by the court (much as the Secretary of State at present approves placement of under-13-year-olds in secure accommodation). The Agency would work collaboratively with local authorities and other relevant people in finding alternative solutions for those children it did not consider should be locked up.

In other words the National Agency would assume some of the responsibilities secure unit managers are currently shouldering for filtering and rejecting unsuitable candidates for a secure place. The advantage to local authorities would be that responsibility for risk-taking would be shared: to an extent the panel would protect local authorities from political considerations and from media criticism. As suggested by the discussion group it could also initi-ate much needed research on risk assessment.

At present, of course, such an undertaking would be difficult given the numbers of children involved. However those organisations (such as The Children's Society and NACRO) which have attempted to calculate how many children would need to be locked up if adequate alternative provision was in place end up with around estimates of around 500 children in all.

The Government has already signalled that **mental health services for children** are now at the top of its priorities, with good reason. Department of Health-sponsored research[19] shows that there is a great deal of dissatisfaction in social services departments with the contribution made by mental health profes-sionals. The bitter comments of the discussion group suggest that health professionals are failing to meet the needs of some of the most troubled children in the country; work by The Children's Society vividly demonstrates the irrational and disjointed response by the four main services (health, education, social ser-vices and youth justice) to dangerous or self-harming children.[20]

Nonetheless many of the children in secure units, particularly those engaged in self-destructive behaviour, clearly lack mental health and mental health services for this group of children need to be rethought as a matter of urgency.

The health services should seize the initiative, and the responsibility, for helping all children who are not mentally well and for working as equal partners with the other agencies (the development of Children's Services Plans and joint commissioning should hopefully improve collaboration). Where a child needs to be detained because of self-harm this could more often be done under mental health legislation (once a child needs to be locked up worries about 'stigma', such as the 'stigma of mental illness' become pretty academic since all forms of locking up are deeply stigmatising).

This is not necessarily saying that any more adolescent psychiatric unit places are needed. As with secure units it can be argued that many children in such units could be better treated at home or within the community. Health professionals should direct their energies into securing the right responses to dangerous or self-harming children in other settings, including children's homes or residential schools but most particularly, of course, within the child's home.

The shape of secure accommodation

Anyone proposing to reform secure accommodation must face the fact that, if it is to act as a last resort and as an effective rehabilitative measure, it cannot come cheap. However the drastic reduction in numbers arising from the legislative and administrative changes proposed above should make the high financial cost of an individual place more palatable.

To date lock-ups for children have grown up in a piecemeal and unthought-out fashion. A systematic review and reorganisation of the whole system, across the penal, social services, health and education sectors, is urgently needed. It is recommended such a review should consider the following proposals:

- children who need to be locked up should be divided into three groups – dangerous children, children on remand and self-destructive children;
- these three groups should not, as a general principle, be accommodated together (although the National Agency would have to retain some discretion over this in order to meet the complex needs of children who, for example, might need to be

placed near home or who belonged to more than one of these groups);

- further specialisation within these categories should be pursued as appropriate;
- social services and health services should be mandated to take joint responsibility for these children and to work collaboratively with each other, so that the health needs and the social services needs of the children would be addressed. (All locked-up children should be subject to the oversight of the courts and the National Agency, see above);
- all locked units should be part of a clear continuum of provision to allow for speedy transfer from locked accommodation to open. It should be accepted that, in the first stages of transition back into the community the open accommodation will cost at least as much as the locked accommodation;
- all locked units should be costed on a low 'notional occupancy' rate of say 60-70%. This would firstly allow the unit some flexibility over moderating its intake to meet the needs of the children it was already accommodating and secondly would reflect the fact that, if small numbers of children are to be genuinely locked up only as a last resort, their numbers are likely to fluctuate;
- all locked units for children should be managed by the National Agency (see above) in collaboration with local authorities and health authorities. The private and voluntary sector would be prohibited from locking up children, as would education authorities.

8. Summary of conclusions

It should first be stated that these proposals are not necessarily the firm recommendations of the National Children's Bureau, they are rather the **preliminary conclusions** arising from the findings of this report (and other Bureau research). The firm recommendation at this point is:

> **That the Government should, as a matter of urgency, convene a major review of all law and policy (penal, health and social services) relating to the locking up of children with a view to securing the aim of Article 37 of the UN Convention on the Rights of the Child – that the child should be locked up only as a last resort and for the shortest appropriate time.**

There are of course a number of questions raised by this report which imply a need for more information and further research, for example exploring why certain groups appear to be treated unevenly or discovering more about the distribution of children (including their class, gender, ethnicity and geographical location) across the various establishments and disciplines involved.

Preliminary conclusions:

- Locked placements for children run by the Home Office in the penal sector should be abandoned.
- Ring-fenced funding should be provided for preventive or community-based alternatives to locked or institutional placements for dangerous, offending or self-harming children.
- Local authorities should be placed under statutory duties to provide or secure the provision of a specified list of such services.
- Local education authorities and health authorities should be placed under a statutory duty to assist the social services in the planning and commissioning of such services and in drawing up strategies to reduce children's anti-social or self-destructive behaviour.

- Schemes to involve in disposals those most affected by the behaviour – particularly victims, parents and the young offender – should be explored and piloted.
- The legal criteria for placement in secure units should be amended along the following lines:
  - 'Likely to injure others if kept in any unlocked accommodation' should be the primary ground for restricting children's liberty. The court should set maximum periods of detention but the child should be eligible for release before then if the criterion no longer applies.
  - Remanded children should in addition be locked up if this is the only means of securing their appearance in court or preventing them from perverting the course of justice.
  - Children likely to injure themselves should only be locked up if this is necessary to protect life or limb or if the behaviour can be alleviated by treatment in the locked unit.
  - The court should consider the plans for discharging children at the same time as hearing the application to lock them up.
- In addition to a court hearing, a central 'National Agency' should be set up to approve and oversee all placements of children in locked accommodation in order to ensure that children are locked up only as a last resort and for the shortest possible time. The Agency would be responsible for resourcing alternative provision and for collaborating with local authorities and other relevant agencies in finding alternative solutions for children who were not approved for a locked placement.
- Social services and health authorities should be given joint responsibility for the locking up of children and should be mandated to work collaboratively together.
- Children who have to be locked up because they are dangerous, because they are on remand and because they are self-destructive should not, as a general principle, be accommodated together.
- All locked units should be managed by the 'National Agency'. Their provision should be costed on a low notional occupancy rate and on providing a continuum of unlocked but potentially very intensive care on discharge.
- The private and voluntary sectors, local education authorities and private medical units should be prohibited from locking up children.

References

1 Home Affairs Select Committee (1993) *Juvenile Offenders Vol 1.* HMSO
2 Boswell G, (1992) *Waiting For a Change.* The Prince's Trust
   Millham S, Bullock R, Hosie K, Little M (1989) *The Experience and Careers of Young People Leaving Youth Treatment Centres.* Dartington Research Unit
3 Herbert M (1987) *Conduct Disorders of Childhood and Adolescence.* Wiley
4 Department of Health (1994) *Children Accommodated in Secure Units During the Year Ending 31 March 1994.* The Government Statistical Service
5 Department of Health (1991) *The Children Act 1989 Guidance and Regulations Volume 4, Residential Care.* HMSO
6 Jaffa and Deszery (1989) 'Reasons for Admission to an Adolescent Unit', *Journal of Adolescence 12*
7 Malek M (1991) *Psychiatric Admissions – a report on young people entering residential psychiatric care.* The Children's Society
8 Clarke R and Martin D (1971) *Absconding From Approved Schools.* HMSO
   Millham S, Bullock R and Hosie K (1978) *Locking Up Children.* Saxon House
9 McGillvray M (1993) *Putting the Brakes on Car Crime.* The Children's Society and Mid Glamorgan County Council
10 (1993) *Awaiting Trial. A survey of juveniles remanded to custody while awaiting trial in criminal proceedings April 1992-March 1993.* NACRO
11 Hagel A and Newburn T (1994) *Persistent Young Offenders.* PSI
12 *The Observer.* 20 November 1994
13 *Hansard.* Written Answers, 1 March 1995, p 576.

14 Cawson P and Martell M (1979) *Children Referred to Locked Units*. HMSO
Millham S *in* Millham S, Bullock R and Hosie K (op. cit.)
15 Harris R and Timms N (1992) *Secure Accommodation in Child Care – between hospital and prison or thereabouts?* Routledge
16 Hoghughi M (1978) *Troubled and Troublesome*. Burnett Books
17 National Association of Guardians ad Litem and Reporting Officers (1992) *Applications for Secure Accommodation Orders*. IFC Press
18 See note 10
(1993) *A False Sense of Security: the case against locking up more children*. The Children's Society.
(1994) *Counting the Cost – an alternative strategy to Secure Training Centres*. NCH-Action for Children
19 Kurtz Z, Thornes R and Wolkind S (1994) *Services for the Mental Health of Children and Young People in England: a national review*. South Thames Regional Health Authority, Department of Public Health
20 Malek M (1993) *Passing the Buck – institutional responses to controlling children with difficult behaviour*. The Children's Society

Appendix: the survey questionnaire

Information on the secure unit

1. Secure unit name and address
2. Name of officer completing the survey (for small establishments this should be the principal officer, for larger units please specify if delegated to the head of subsection).
3. What is the Statement of Purpose of your secure unit (as required under the Children's Homes Regulations)? Please attach, if appropriate.
4. Is the secure unit attached to on-site provision?
5. How many young people were accommodated in the secure unit on 31 March 1994?
6. How many places were available on 31 March 1994?

Information on the young person

1. Date of birth
2. Sex
3. Ethnic category (White, Black Caribbean, Black African, Black other, Indian, Pakistani, Bangladeshi, Chinese, Other – please specify, Mixed parentage – please specify)
4. Date of admission to the unit
5. Has he or she been in the secure unit before? If yes, please list periods of previous placements.
6. What is the name of the care authority (if appropriate)?

Section 25

7.1 What is the young person's legal status?:
   - Received into care (s2 CCA 80) or accommodated (s20 CA 89)
   - Subject to care in care proceedings

- Subject to care in criminal proceedings or supervision order with residence requirement
- remanded to care under Section 23 of the CYPA 69, but not subject to the amended criteria under Regulations 6 of the Children (Secure Accommodation) Regulations 1991 (i.e. charged with or convicted of serious offences etc).
- ward of court
- other

7.2 Date on which the current secure order is made:

7.3 For what period was the order made?

7.4 At the time of admission, under which of the following grounds of Section 25 were you informed that the secure placement was authorised? (More than one ground may apply):

(a) 'That he has a history of absconding and is likely to abscond from any other description of accommodation and if he absconds is likely to suffer significant harm'. If yes:

(i) what was the history of absconding?

(ii) why did it appear that he or she was likely to abscond from 'any other description of accommodation'

(iii) what significant harm was he/she likely to suffer?

(b) 'That if kept in any other description of accommodation he is likely to injure himself'. If yes:

(i) why did it appear 'no other description of accommodation' was able to prevent the self-injury?

(ii) in what way was s/he likely to injure her/himself?

(c) 'That if kept in any other description of accommodation he is likely to injure other persons'. If yes:

(i) why did it appear 'no other description of accommodation' was able to prevent the injury to other persons?

(ii) in what way was s/he likely to injure other persons?

7.5 What was the source of this information?

7.6 Have these grounds changed since admission? If yes, how?

7.7 **In your opinion**, could the young person have been placed safely in some form of 'other description of accommodation' when he or she was admitted to the unit. If yes, what sort of other accommodation?

7.8 **In your opinion,** could the young person now be placed safely in some form of 'other description of accommodation'? If yes, what sort of other accommodation?

Regulation 6

8.1 What is the young person's legal status:
- detained under Section 38(6) of the PACE 1984
- remanded to local authority accommodation under Section 23 of the CYPA 1969 and charged with or convicted of a serious, sexual or violent offence, or with a recent history of absconding and been charged with or convicted of an imprisonable offence alleged or found to have been committed while on remand
- other

8.2 On what date was the current secure order made?

8.3 For what period was the order made?

8.4 At the time of admission under which of the following grounds of Regulation 6 was the secure placement authorised?
  (a) 'Unless it appears that any accommodation other than that provided for the purpose of restricting liberty is inappropriate because the child is likely to abscond from such other accommodation'. If yes:
    (i) What (if any) 'other accommodation' had the child been placed in?
    (ii) Why was he likely to abscond?
    (iii) Was this absconding likely to mean that the young person would not attend court for trial or sentencing?
  (b) 'likely to injure himself if he is kept in such other accommodation'. If yes:
    (i) Why did it appear 'other accommodation' could not prevent the self-injury?
    (ii) In what way was s/he likely to injure him/herself?
  (c) 'likely to injure other persons if he is kept in such other accommodation'. If yes:
    (i) Why did it appear no 'other accommodation' was able to prevent the injury to other persons?
    (ii) In what way was s/he likely to injure other persons?

8.5 What was the source of this information?

8.6 Have these grounds changed since admission? If yes, how?

8.7 **In your opinion**, could the young person have been placed safely in some form of 'other accommodation' when s/he was admitted to the unit?

8.8 **In your opinion**, could the young person now be placed safely in some form of 'other accommodation'. If yes, what sort of other accommodation?

Section 53

9.1 What is the young person's legal status:
- Section 53(1)
- Section 53(2)
9.2 On what date was the sentence passed?
9.3 How long was the sentence?
9.4 On what date was the young person placed at the unit?
9.5 What offence did the young person commit?

Under Section 53 the Home Secretary has discretion to place the young person in open provision:
9.6 **In your opinion**, at the time of admission do you think the young person could have been safely accommodated in some sort of open provision? If yes, what sort of open provision?
9.7 **In your opinion**, do you think the young person could now be safely accommodated in some sort of open provision? If yes, what sort of open provision?

Becoming a member

The National Children's Bureau offers an extensive Library and Information Service – probably the largest child care information resource in the UK. We also run a comprehensive programme of conferences and seminars, and publish a wide range of books, leaflets and resource packs. In addition, the Bureau gives members the opportunity to tap into an influential network of professionals who care about children, helping to set the agenda for the nineties and beyond.

Membership of the National Children's Bureau provides you with:

- a quarterly mailing containing:
  - *Children UK*: the Bureau's journal
  - *Highlights:* briefing papers containing summaries of research findings and recent reports of legislation on relevant issues;
- access to the library and information service including databases, books, journals and periodicals;
- first access to the findings of our research and development projects;
- advance notice of our extensive programme of conferences and seminars throughout the country and concessionary prices;
- concessionary prices and advance details for Bureau publications.

The National Children's Bureau can support you in the day to day task of meeting the needs of children and young people. For further details please contact Jane Lewis, Membership Marketing Coordinator, National Children's Bureau, 8 Wakley Street, London EC1V 7QE or call 0171 843 6047 for further information.

Publications

Recent works include:

Day Nurseries at a Crossroads
Meeting the Challenge of Child Care in the Nineties

Developing a School Sex Education Policy: A positive strategy

Educating Disruptive Children
Placement and progress in residential special schools for pupils with emotional and behavioural difficulties

The Future Shape of Children's Services

Children and Residential Care in Europe

For further information or a catalogue please contact:
Book Sales, National Children's Bureau, 8 Wakley Street, London EC1V 7QE
Tel: 0171 843 6029   Fax: 0171 278 9512